GRADE 8

The Syllabus of Examinations should be read for details of requirements, especially those for scales, aural tests and sight-reading. Attention s[illegible]ld be paid to the Special Notices on the front [illegible]er, where warning is given of changes.

The syllabus is obtain[illegible]rs or from The Associated Board [illegible] 14 Bedford Square, L[illegible] stamped addressed C5 [illegible]

In centres outside the UK, [illegible] obtained from the Local Repres[illegible]

REQUIREMENTS

SCALES AND ARPEGGIOS (from memory)

Scales legato or staccato, as directed by the examiner:
(i) in similar motion, hands together one octave apart, and each hand separately, in the following keys (minors in melodic *and* harmonic forms) (four octaves): C, D, B, F♯, F, E♭, A♭, D♭ majors and minors
(ii) in similar motion, hands together a third apart, and a sixth apart, in the major and harmonic minor keys set for (i) (four octaves)
(iii) legato *only*, in thirds, each hand separately, in the keys of C and B♭ majors (two octaves)

Chromatic Scales legato or staccato, as directed by the examiner:
(i) in similar motion, hands together a minor third apart, beginning on any note named by the examiner (four octaves)
(ii) legato *only*, each hand separately, in minor thirds beginning on A♯/C♯ (two octaves)

Arpeggios legato *only*, hands together one octave apart, and each hand separately:
(i) the common chords, in root position, first and second inversions of the keys set for the scales (i) (four octaves)
(ii) dominant seventh chords, in root position *only*, in the keys set for the scales (i) (four octaves)
(iii) diminished seventh chords, beginning on any note (four octaves)

PLAYING AT SIGHT (see current syllabus)

AURAL TESTS (see current syllabus)

Candidates must prepare three pieces, one from each of the three Lists, A, B and C. Candidates may choose from the pieces printed in this volume or any other piece listed for the grade. Full lists are given in the syllabus and on the inside covers of the *Selected Piano Examination Pieces, 1999–2000.*

THREE PIECES

Editor for the Associated Board: **Richard Jones**

Music origination by Barnes Music Engraving Ltd.
Printed in Great Britain by Headley Brothers Ltd, The Invicta Press, Ashford, Kent

Where appropriate, pieces have been checked with original source material and edited as necessary for instructional purposes. Fingering, phrasing, pedalling, metronome marks and the editorial realization of ornaments (where given) are for guidance but are not comprehensive or obligatory.

A:1

Gigue & Menuet

Last two movements from French Suite No. 6 in E, BWV 817

J. S. BACH

Gigue
[♩. = c.66]

Sources: Staatsbibliothek zu Berlin, Preussischer Kulturbesitz, Mus. ms. Bach P 420 & 1221.

Selected from J. S. Bach, *French Suites, BWV 812–817*, edited by Richard Jones (Associated Board)

13
16
19
22

25
28
31
34

37
40
43
46

Menuet

[♩ = *c.*120]

Fugue in E minor

A:2

Op. 84 No. 6

FAURÉ

Source: *Pièces brèves pour piano*, Op. 84 (Paris, Hamelle, 1903).

p
cresc. poco a
poco
f

f
f sempre
poco a poco
cresc.
f
poco rit.
dim.
p

A:3

Sonata in C

Pastorale
Kp. 513

D. SCARLATTI

Source: Parma XIV 30. Since it is self-explanatory, the inexact notation of bb. 13–15, R.H., has been retained.

Molto allegro
[♩. = *c.*84]

Presto [♩. = c.76]

58
63
68
72
77

B:1

Allegro Assai

First movement from Sonata in A, H. 18b, Wq. 55/4

C. P. E. BACH

Allegro assai [♩ = *c.*112]

Source: *Sechs Clavier-Sonaten für Kenner und Liebhaber . . Erste Sammlung* (Leipzig, Author, 1779), No. 4. The first two movements of Sonata No. 4 are joined by a transition. The second-time bar, b. 121b, which allows the first movement to be played as an independent piece, is, in this edition, editorial.

In passages divided between the hands (bb. 9–11 etc.), upstems indicate R.H. and downstems L.H.

R
L
f
p

31
f
34
37
p
pp
41
f
1
2
43
[f]
p
f
p
47
f

R
L

69
ff
72
75
p
ff
79
82
p
f
p
86
f

89
92
95
98
100

102
p
f
105
p
109
f
112
115
p
119
pp
f

Allegro

B:2

First movement from Sonata in E, Op. 14 No. 1

BEETHOVEN

Source: *Deux Sonates pour le Piano-Forte,* Op. 14 (Bonn, Simrock, 1800). Small inconsistencies in the length of slurs have been corrected by the editor.

p
[p]
p
p

44
rfz
rfz
f
f
48
rfz
rfz
f
f
p
52
cresc.
rfz
f
rfz
56
p
pp
60
[p]
1
2

[cantabile]
63
cresc.
[fp]
66
69
cresc.
p
cresc.
72
rfz
75
p
pp
78
cresc.
rfz

81
p
85
89
decresc.
f
92
rfz
95
p
98
decresc.

pp
cresc.
f
p
rfz

132
137
rfz
f
p
142
cresc.
ff
148
pp
153
158
decresc.

B:3

Moderato

First movement from Sonata in C sharp minor, Hob. XVI/36

HAYDN

Source: *Sei Sonate per il Clavicembalo, o Forte Piano*, Op. 30 (Vienna, Artaria, 1780), No. 2. The sign *fz* appears in the source as *f* or *ff*. The slurs in bb. 12–13 are inaccurately placed and have been corrected here according to b. 14.

Players might consider dotting the rhythms in bb. 95–6 in accordance with those of bb. 31–2.

[f]
p
p
f
p
f

56
59
62
66
71
74
76

fz
fz
fz
[fz]
dolce
p
f
[fz]
p

Intermezzo in E

C:1

Op. 116 No. 6

Edited by
Howard Ferguson

BRAHMS

Andantino teneramente [tenderly; ♩ = *c.*69]

[Poco più mosso; ♩ = c.88]
p dolce
p [sub.]
f
p
sost.
cresc.
rit. molto
f
p dim.
[Tempo primo]
pp dolce

Source: *Fantasien für Pianoforte*, Op. 116 (Berlin, Simrock, 1892), Brahms's *Handexemplar*, Vienna, Gesellschaft der Musikfreunde.

The third R.H. chord in b. 19 may be played thus by small hands:

The second R.H. chord in b. 22 coincides with the lowest note of the L.H. arpeggio. Brahms's own fingering for the L.H. triplet in b. 57 is 512; the editor has substituted 521 to facilitate the fingering of the following chord.

Suggested execution of the first chord in b. 60:

and of the last chord in the piece:

Reprinted from Brahms, *Seven Fantasies, Op. 116*, edited by Howard Ferguson (Associated Board)

C:2

Général Lavine – eccentric

No. 6 from *Préludes*, Book II

DEBUSSY

Source: *Préludes pour piano, 2me livre* (Paris, Durand, 1913), No. 6.

17
sff
sff sec
22
27
molto staccato
molto cresc.

31
R
L
36
R
41
R

Traîné [dragging]
Mouvt [in time]
46
p
51
f
p
pp
R
L
pp
57
Traîné
Mouvt
ff
p subito
L
sff

62
f
Très retenu
67
ff
f
Mouvt
p
pp
[p]
73
R
L
sff
sff sec
8va basso

78
p
pp
[pp]
R
84
[molto staccato]
molto cresc.
89
f
R
3

Très retenu
Animez
cresc.
sff sec

Nocturne No. 4 in A

C:3

FIELD

Source: *Quatrième Notturno pour le pianoforte* (St. Petersburg, Lissner, *c.*1816/17).

dolce
cresc.
dim.
piangendo

29
poco f
dim.
31
fz
33
35
37
p
cresc.
39
41
f
dim.

43
fz p
dim.
45
P
47
dim.
rall.
49
dim.
a tempo
51
p [dolce]
[dim.]
54
ppp
delicatiss. pp

[mf]
espress.
[p]
[pp]
morendo
[a tempo]
rit.
poco f
perdendosi
8va

C:4

The Cherry Tree

from *Greenways: Three Lyric Pieces for Piano*

Moderato e con grazia [♪ = *c.*120]

IRELAND

Source: *Greenways: Three Lyric Pieces for Piano* (London, Winthrop Rogers, 1938), No. 1. The piece carries a dedication to Herbert S. Brown. Underneath the title Ireland has appended a verse by A. E. Housman: And since to look at things in bloom / Fifty springs are little room, / About the woodlands I will go / To see the cherry hung with snow.

15
f
mf
17
p
p
20
23
mf
cresc.
f
26
8va
ten.
P

p delicato
28
mp
pochiss. rit.
31
p
mp
33
p
ten.
8va
35
p
mp
p
P

Improvisation No. 13 in A minor

C:5

POULENC

Source: *XIII*[ème] *improvisation en la mineur* (Paris, Salabert, 1958). This piece was written at Cannes in March 1958 and dedicated to Madame Auguste Lambiotte.

m.g. en dehors
rit.
a tempo
très expressif

molto
en dehors
(dessus)
[over]
céder beaucoup
Très lent
8va basso

C:6

Bagatelle No. 4

from *Five Bagatelles*

CARL VINE

Source: *Five Bagatelles* (London, Faber, 1995), No. 4.
In bb. 29–31 '*8:6*' instructs the pianist to play eight semiquavers in the time of six.

ff
mf
sim.
p sub.
12
15
pp
p
18
22

ff
25
sim.
27
29
p
pp
8:6
ppp
8va
a tempo
32
(RH forearm
black-note cluster)